THIS JOURNAL BELONGS TO

_____

THE
PEACE
JOURNAL

A Personal Book of
Inspiration, Contemplation
and Courage

st. lynn's
press

PITTSBURGH

The Peace Journal
A Personal Book of Inspiration, Contemplation and Courage

Copyright © 2008 by St. Lynn's Press

Grateful acknowledgment is given to The Nobel Foundation for permission to present excerpts from Nobel Peace Laureate lectures.

ISBN-13: 978-0-9800288-1-2

Library of Congress Control Number: 2008922293
CIP information available upon request

First Edition, 2008

St. Lynn's Press . POB 18680 . Pittsburgh, PA 15236
412.466.0790 . www.stlynnspress.com

Typesetting—Holly Wensel, Network Printing Services
Cover design—Jeff Nicoll
Cover Calligraphy—Sandra Bruce
Editors—Catherine Dees, Abby Dees

Printed in the United States of America
on recycled paper ♲

This title and all of St. Lynn's Press books may be purchased for educational, business, or sales promotional use. For information please write:
Special Markets Department . St. Lynn's Press . POB 18680 . Pittsburgh, PA 15236

10 9 8 7 6 5 4 3 2 1

Out beyond ideas of wrongdoing and rightdoing
There is a field. I'll meet you there.

Rumi
(trans. Coleman Barks)

About the Journal

"All works of love are works of peace," Mother Teresa said. She also said, "Do not wait for leaders; do it alone, person to person." Her life was a testament to the power of a single determined individual to create peace with every touch, smile and word – by simply "doing it."

Scattered in the pages of this journal you will encounter the words of dozens of other courageous individuals who didn't wait for leaders, but spoke and acted for peace, person to person, in ways small and large. Many of them were recipients of the Nobel Peace Prize for their larger works, yet beneath their varied accomplishments runs a grand unifying theme of love: love of justice, love of humanity, love of the earth – and the conviction that no act is too small to matter when it is done in the name of love.

We hope you will find the voices of these women and men inspiring and encouraging as you create your own path of peace.

The Editors

MONTH

Peace is always
beautiful.

Walt Whitman

I believe that every
one of us aspires to
peace — in our family,
community, nation
and the world. If we
come together and sit
down calmly, we realize
that to attain peace
we must be peace.
The way we walk, talk,
eat, present ourselves,
resolve difficulties,
should be peace.
...There is no way
to peace.
Peace is the way.

Thich Nhat Hanh

It isn't enough to talk about peace. One must believe in it. And it isn't enough to believe in it. One must work at it.

Eleanor Roosevelt

Peace is not unity
in similarity but
unity in diversity,
in the comparison
and conciliation
of differences.

≈

Mikhail Gorbachev

How wonderful it is
that nobody need
wait a single moment
before starting to
improve the world.

Anne Frank

Of one thing I am
certain: The body is
not the measure of
healing, peace is
the measure.

Phyllis McGinley

Frederik Willem de Klerk

Former President of the Republic of South Africa
From his Nobel Lecture given in Oslo, December 1993

Peace does not simply mean the absence of conflict.

Throughout history, there has been an absence of conflict in many repressive societies. This lack of conflict does not have its roots in harmony, goodwill or the consent of the parties involved – but often in fear, ignorance and powerlessness. There can thus be no real peace without justice or consent.

Neither does peace necessarily imply tranquility.

The affairs of mankind are in incessant flux. No relationship – between individuals or communities or political parties or countries – remains the same from one day to the next. New situations are forever arising and demand constant attention. Tensions build up and need to be defused. Militant radical minorities plan to disrupt peace and need to be contained.

There can thus be no real peace without constant effort, planning and hard work. Peace, therefore, is not an absence of conflict or a condition of stagnation.

Peace is a frame of mind.

It is a frame of mind in which countries, communities, parties and individuals seek to resolve their differences through agreements, through negotiation and compromise, instead of threats, compulsion and violence.

It is a framework consisting of rules, laws, agreements and conventions – a framework providing mechanisms for the peaceful resolution of the inevitable clashes of interest between countries, communities, parties and individuals. It is a framework within which the irresistible and dynamic processes of social, economic and political development can be regulated and accommodated.

MONTH

Peace is not an
absence of war, it
is a virtue, a state of
mind, a disposition
for benevolence,
confidence, justice.

Baruch Spinoza

If we have not peace,
it is because we have
forgotten that we
belong to each other.

Mother Teresa

No man is an Iland,
intire of it selfe;
every man is a peece
of the Continent,
a part of the Maine.

John Donne

[L]iberty without responsibility is not true liberty. We are not free to destroy.

Thich Nhat Hanh

It is no moral excuse to
wring your hands and
cry, "But I never knew"
— if you never asked
to know.

❧

*International Campaign
to Ban Landmines*

> None who have
> always been free
> can understand the
> terrible fascinating
> power of the hope
> of freedom to those
> who are not free.
>
> *Pearl S. Buck*

Elie Wiesel

Author, Holocaust Survivor and Co-Founder of
the Elie Wiesel Foundation for Humanity
From his Nobel Lecture given in Oslo, December 11, 1986

For us, forgetting was never an option.

Remembering is a noble and necessary act. The call of memory, the call to memory, reaches us from the very dawn of history. No commandment figures so frequently, so insistently, in the Bible. It is incumbent upon us to remember the good we have received, and the evil we have suffered. New Year's Day, Rosh Hashana, is also called Yom Hazikaron, the day of memory. On that day, the day of universal judgment, man appeals to God to remember: Our salvation depends on it. If God wishes to remember our suffering, all will be well; if He refuses, all will be lost. Thus, the rejection of memory becomes a divine curse, one that would doom us to repeat past disasters, past wars.

Nothing provokes so much horror and opposition within the Jewish tradition as war. Our abhorrence of war is reflected in the paucity of our literature of warfare. After all, God created the Torah to do away with iniquity, to do away with war. Warriors fare poorly in the Talmud: Judas Maccabeus is not even mentioned; Bar-Kochba is cited, but negatively. David, a great warrior and conqueror, is not permitted to build the Temple; it is his son Solomon, a man of peace, who constructs God's dwelling place. Of course some wars may have been necessary or inevitable, but none was ever regarded as holy. For us, a holy war is a contradiction in terms. War dehumanizes, war diminishes, war debases all those who wage it. The Talmud says, "Talmidei hukhamim shemarbin shalom baolam" (It is the wise men who will bring about peace). Perhaps, because wise men remember best. ...

MONTH

Who are we if we are
not useful to others?

Angelina Jolie

How can one not speak
about war, poverty, and
inequality when people
who suffer from these
afflictions don't have
a voice to speak?

Isabel Allende

Until he extends the
circle of his compassion
to all living things,
man will not himself
find peace.

~

Albert Schweitzer

This we know: The earth does not belong to man — man belongs to the earth. This we know: All things are connected like the blood which unites one family. All things are connected. Whatever befalls the earth befalls the sons of the earth.

Chief Seattle

Love all God's creation,
the whole and every
grain of sand in it. Love
every leaf, every ray of
God's light. Love the
animals, love the plants,
love everything. If you
love everything, you
will perceive the divine
mystery in things. Once
you perceive it, you will
come at last to love the
whole world with an
all-embracing love.

Feodor Dostoevsky

It is clear to me that
unless we connect
directly with the earth,
we will not have the
faintest clue why we
should save it.

Dr. Helen Caldicott

Wangari Maathai

Founder of the Green Belt Movement, in Kenya
From her Nobel Lecture given in Oslo, Dec 10, 2004

[T]he state of any country's environment is a reflection of the kind of governance in place, and without good governance there can be no peace. Many countries which have poor governance systems are also likely to have conflicts and poor laws protecting the environment. ...

Today we are faced with a challenge that calls for a shift in our thinking, so that humanity stops threatening its life-support system. We are called to assist the Earth to heal her wounds and in the process heal our own – indeed, to embrace the whole creation in all its diversity, beauty and wonder. This will happen if we see the need to revive our sense of belonging to a larger family of life, with which we have shared our evolutionary process.

In the course of history, there comes a time when humanity is called to shift to a new level of consciousness, to reach a higher moral ground. A time when we have to shed our fear and give hope to each other.

That time is now.

The Norwegian Nobel Committee has challenged the world to broaden the understanding of peace: There can be no peace without equitable development; and there can be no development without sustainable management of the environment in a democratic and peaceful space. This shift is an idea whose time has come.

The Green Belt Movement was founded to preserve the natural resources of Kenya and beyond, and to empower women as agents of environmental sustainability. In just over 30 years, the Green Belt Movement has planted 40 million trees.

MONTH

Surely, it's better to
love others, however
messy and imperfect the
involvement, than to
allow one's capacity
for love to harden.

Karen Armstrong

If we could read the secret history of our enemies, we should find in each man's life sorrow and suffering enough to disarm all hostility.

Henry Wadsworth Longfellow

All creatures are like a family of God; and He loves the most those who are the most beneficent to His family.

A saying (hadith) of Mohammed

Doing an injury puts
you below your enemy;
Revenging one makes
you but even with him;
Forgiving it sets you
above him.

Ben Franklin,
Poor Richard's Almanac

Non-violence doesn't
always work – but
violence never does.

Madge Michaels-Cyrus

Security is mostly a superstition. It does not exist in nature, nor do the children of men as a whole experience it. Avoiding danger is no safer in the long run than outright exposure. Life is either a daring adventure, or nothing. To keep our faces toward change and behave like free spirits in the presence of fate is strength undefeatable.

Helen Keller

prayer of saint francis

O Lord, make me an instrument of Thy peace;
where there is hatred, let me sow love;
where there is injury, pardon;
where there is doubt, faith;
where there is despair, hope;
where there is darkness, light;
and where there is sadness, joy.

O Divine Master,
grant that I may not so much seek to be consoled as to console;
to be understood, as to understand;
to be loved, as to love;
for it is in giving that we receive,
it is in pardoning that we are pardoned,
and it is in dying that we are born to eternal life.
Amen.

Author Unknown

MONTH

One does not need
buildings, money, power,
or status to practice the
Art of Peace. Heaven
is right where you are
standing, and that is
the place to train.

Morihei Ueshiba

No pessimist ever
discovered the secrets
of the stars, or sailed to
an uncharted land, or
opened a new heaven
to the human spirit.

Helen Keller

To go against the
dominant thinking of
your friends, of most of
the people you see every
day, is perhaps the most
difficult act of heroism
you can have.

Theodore H. White

Whatever you do, you need courage. Whatever course you decide upon, there is always someone to tell you that you are wrong. There are always difficulties arising that tempt you to believe your critics are right. To map out a course of action and follow it to an end requires some of the same courage that a soldier needs. Peace has its victories, but it takes brave men and women to win them.

Ralph Waldo Emerson

A soul is known
by its acts.

St. Thomas Aquinas

Peace is not abstract;
on the contrary, it must
have profound social,
political, economic,
and cultural substance.
...I believe that peace is
a condition, an essential
requirement for the
survival of humankind.

Rigoberta Menchú Tum

Al Gore

Former Vice President of the United States
From his Nobel Lecture given in Oslo, December 10, 2007

The way ahead is difficult. The outer boundary of what we currently believe is feasible is still far short of what we actually must do. Moreover, between here and there, across the unknown, falls the shadow.

That is just another way of saying that we have to expand the boundaries of what is possible. In the words of the Spanish poet, Antonio Machado, "Pathwalker, there is no path. You must make the path as you walk."

We are standing at the most fateful fork in that path. So I want to end as I began, with a vision of two futures – each a palpable possibility – and with a prayer that we will see with vivid clarity the necessity of choosing between those two futures, and the urgency of making the right choice now.

The great Norwegian playwright, Henrik Ibsen, wrote, "One of these days, the younger generation will come knocking at my door." The future is knocking at our door right now. Make no mistake, the next generation will ask us one of two questions. Either they will ask: "What were you thinking; why didn't you act? "

Or they will ask instead: "How did you find the moral courage to rise and successfully resolve a crisis that so many said was impossible to solve?"

We have everything we need to get started, save perhaps political will, but political will is a renewable resource. So let us renew it, and say together: "We have a purpose. We are many. For this purpose we will rise, and we will act."

In recognizing Al Gore for his work on global warming, the Nobel Committee affirmed the profound connection between peace and environmental stewardship.

MONTH

> God gives us the
> capacity for choice.
> We can choose to
> alleviate suffering. We
> can choose to work
> together for peace.
> We can make these
> changes – we must.
>
> *Jimmy Carter*

Weapons don't fire on their own. Those who have lost hope fire them. Those who are controlled by dogmas fire them.*

∾

Oscar Arias Sánchez

There will be change, because all the military have are guns.

∾

Aung San Suu Kyi

I find it amazing that the only population that does not kill, rape or pillage during war are often the same group that is left out of the peace-building process. It is necessary to understand how women create peace in time of war if we are to build just and peaceful societies after the bombs have stopped falling. To paraphrase Rumi: Out beyond the ideas of war and peace there is a field, and women are meeting there.

Zainab Salbi, Co-founder, Women For Women International

Gandhi taught that
nonviolence does not
mean passivity. No.
It is the most daring,
creative, and courageous
way of living, and it
is the only hope
for our world.

Mairead Corrigan Maguire

I am fragile, delicate,
and sensitive. That
is my strength.

Osho

> You gain strength, courage, and confidence by every experience in which you really stop to look fear in the face. You must do the thing which you think you cannot do.
>
> *Eleanor Roosevelt*

Betty Williams

Co-Founder of Community of Peace People, in Northern Ireland
From her Nobel Lecture given in Oslo, December 11, 1977

War has traditionally been a man's work, although we know that often women were the cause of violence. But the voice of women, the voice of those most closely involved in bringing forth new life, has not always been listened to when it pleaded and implored against the waste of life in war after war. The voice of women has a special role and a special soul force in the struggle for a nonviolent world. ...

So we are honored, in the name of all women, that women have been honored especially for their part in leading a nonviolent movement for a just and peaceful society. Compassion is more important than intellect, in calling forth the love that the work of peace needs, and intuition can often be a far more powerful searchlight than cold reason. We have to think, and think hard, but if we do not have compassion before we even start thinking, then we are quite likely to start fighting over theories. The whole world is divided ideologically, and theologically, right and left, and men are prepared to fight over their ideological differences. Yet the whole human family can be united by compassion. ...

Because of the role of women over so many centuries in so many different cultures, they have been excluded from what have been called public affairs; for that very reason they have concentrated much more on things close to home – and they have kept far more in touch with the true realities, the realities of giving birth and love. The moment has perhaps come in human history when, for very survival, those realities must be given pride of place over the vainglorious adventures that lead to war.

MONTH

You must not lose faith in humanity. Humanity is an ocean; if a few drops of the ocean are dirty, the ocean does not become dirty.

Gandhi

Forgiveness, like other positive emotions such as hope, compassion, and appreciation, are natural expressions of being human. They exist within a deep part of each of us. Like many things, they require practice to perfect. When you practice these positive feelings they become stronger and easier to find. ...Forgiveness can be as natural a response to hurt as are anger and pain.

Fred Luskin, co-founder, the Stanford University Forgiveness Project

We have learned to fly
the air like birds and
swim the sea like fish,
but we have not learned
the simple art of living
together as brothers.

Dr. Martin Luther King, Jr.

[W]e are not going to
deal with the violence
in our communities, our
homes, and our nation,
until we learn to deal
with the basic ethic
of how we resolve our
disputes and to place an
emphasis on peace in
the way we relate to
one another.

Marian Wright Edelman

We believe that justice
and peace can only
thrive together, never
apart. A nation that
mistreats its own
citizens is more likely to
mistreat its neighbors.

≈

Oscar Arias Sánchez

War will stop when we no longer praise it, or give it any attention at all. Peace will come wherever it is sincerely invited.

Alice Walker

Archbishop Desmond Tutu

*First Black General Secretary of the South African Council of Churches
and Founder of the Desmond Tutu Peace Foundation
From his Nobel Lecture given in Oslo, December 1984*

Unless we work assiduously so that all of God's children, our brothers and sisters, members of our one human family, all will enjoy basic human rights, the right to a fulfilled life, the right of movement, of work, the freedom to be fully human, with a humanity measured by nothing less than the humanity of Jesus Christ Himself, then we are on the road inexorably to self-destruction, we are not far from global suicide; and yet it could be so different.

When will we learn that human beings are of infinite value because they have been created in the image of God, and that it is a blasphemy to treat them as if they were less than this and to do so ultimately recoils on those who do this? In dehumanizing others, they are themselves dehumanized. Perhaps oppression dehumanizes the oppressor as much as, if not more than, the oppressed. They need each other to become truly free, to become human. We can be human only in fellowship, in community, in koinonia, in peace.

Let us work to be peacemakers, those given a wonderful share in Our Lord's ministry of reconciliation. If we want peace, so we have been told, let us work for justice. Let us beat our swords into ploughshares.

God calls us to be fellow workers with Him, so that we can extend His Kingdom of Shalom, of justice, of goodness, of compassion, of caring, of sharing, of laughter, joy and reconciliation, so that the kingdoms of this world will become the Kingdom of our God and of His Christ, and He shall reign forever and ever. Amen. …

MONTH

Whatever you do will
be insignificant, but
it is very important
that you do it.

Gandhi

No act of kindness,
no matter how small,
is ever wasted.

Aesop

One day we must come
to see that peace is not
merely a distant goal
we seek, but that it
is a means by which
we arrive at that goal.
We must pursue
peaceful ends through
peaceful means.

Dr. Martin Luther King, Jr.

Establishing lasting
peace is the work of
education; all politics
can do is keep us
out of war.

Maria Montessori

First keep the peace within yourself, then you can also bring peace to others.

Thomas À Kempis

Peace is every step.

Thich Nhat Hanh

Never doubt that a small
group of thoughtful,
committed citizens
can change the world:
Indeed, it's the only
thing that ever has.

Margaret Mead

blessing prayer

Blessed are they who love and trust their fellow human beings, for they shall reach the good in people and receive a loving response.

Blessed are they who translate every good thing they know into action – even higher truths shall be revealed to them.

Blessed are they who, after dedicating their lives and thereby receiving a blessing, have the courage and faith to surmount the difficulties of the path ahead, for they shall receive a second blessing.

Blessed are they who advance toward the spiritual path without the selfish motive of seeking inner peace, for they shall find it.

Peace Pilgrim
Wanderer and Messenger of Peace

MONTH

The topic of unselfish
love has been placed
on the agenda of
history and is about
to become its
main business.

Pitirim Sorokin

If the 21st century
wishes to free itself from
the cycle of violence,
acts of terror and war,
and avoid repetition of
the experience of the
20th century — that
most disaster-ridden
century of humankind,
there is no other way
except by understanding
and putting into practice
every human right
for all mankind,
irrespective of race,
gender, faith, nationality
or social status.

Shirin Ebadi

All know the way, but
few actually walk it.

Bodhidharma

As we are liberated
from our own fear, our
presence automatically
liberates others.

❧

Nelson Mandela

If we learn to open our hearts, anyone, including the people who drive us crazy, can be our teacher.

Pema Chodron

A human being is part
of the whole called
by us the "Universe,"
a part limited in
time and space. He
experiences himself, his
thoughts and feelings
as something separated
from the rest—a kind
of optical delusion of
consciousness. This
delusion is a kind of
prison for us, restricting
us to our personal
desires and to affection
for a few persons nearest
us. Our task must be
to free ourselves from
this prison by widening
our circle of compassion
to embrace all living
creatures and the whole
of nature in its beauty.

Albert Einstein

His Holiness the 14th Dalai Lama

Spiritual leader and exiled head of state of Tibet
From his Nobel Lecture given in Oslo, December 11, 1989

Today, we are truly a global family. What happens in one part of the world may affect us all. ...

[W]ar or peace, the destruction or the protection of nature, the violation or promotion of human rights and democratic freedoms, poverty or material well-being, the lack of moral and spiritual values or their existence and development, and the breakdown or development of human understanding, are not isolated phenomena that can be analyzed and tackled independently of one another. In fact, they are very much interrelated at all levels and need to be approached with that understanding. ...

Responsibility does not only lie with the leaders of our countries or with those who have been appointed or elected to do a particular job. It lies with each one of us individually. Peace, for example, starts with each one of us. When we have inner peace, we can be at peace with those around us. When our community is in a state of peace, it can share that peace with neighboring communities, and so on.

When we feel love and kindness towards others, it not only makes others feel loved and cared for, but it helps us also to develop inner happiness and peace. And there are ways in which we can consciously work to develop feelings of love and kindness. For some of us, the most effective way to do so is through religious practice. For others it may be non-religious practices. What is important is that we each make a sincere effort to take our responsibility for each other and for the natural environment we live in seriously. ...

MONTH

When I speak of love
I am not speaking of
some sentimental and
weak response which
is little more than
emotional bosh. I am
speaking of that force
which all of the great
religions have seen as
the supreme unifying
principle of life.

Dr. Martin Luther King, Jr.

I am prepared to die,
but there is no cause
for which I am
prepared to kill.

Gandhi

Nothing worth doing
is completed in our
lifetime; therefore,
we are saved by hope.
Nothing true or
beautiful or good makes
complete sense in any
immediate context of
history; therefore, we are
saved by faith. Nothing
we do, however virtuous,
can be accomplished
alone; therefore, we
are saved by love. No
virtuous act is quite
as virtuous from the
standpoint of our friend
or foe as from our own;
therefore, we are saved
by the final form of love
which is forgiveness.

Reinhold Niebuhr

We all know that a simple handshake, a simple embrace, can break down enmity between two people. Multiply such acts of friendship all over the world, and then the moments of pathetic friendship in the miserable trenches of the First World War would no longer be the exception but the rule in human affairs.

Betty Williams

I must say a word
about fear. It is life's
only true opponent.
Only fear can defeat life.
...You dismiss your last
allies: hope and trust.
There, you've defeated
yourself. Fear, which is
but an impression, has
triumphed over you.

Yann Martel,
from Life of Pi

This is the way of peace:
overcome evil with
good, and falsehood
with truth, and
hatred with love.

Peace Pilgrim

Martin Luther King, Jr.

Civil rights leader and, at age 35, the youngest person
ever to receive the Nobel Peace Prize
From his acceptance speech given in Oslo, December 10, 1964

...I accept this award today with an abiding faith in America and an audacious faith in the future of mankind. I refuse to accept despair as the final response to the ambiguities of history. I refuse to accept the idea that the "isness" of man's present nature makes him morally incapable of reaching up for the eternal "oughtness" that forever confronts him.

I refuse to accept the idea that man is mere flotsom and jetsom in the river of life unable to influence the unfolding events which surround him. I refuse to accept the view that mankind is so tragically bound to the starless midnight of racism and war that the bright daybreak of peace and brotherhood can never become a reality.

I refuse to accept the cynical notion that nation after nation must spiral down a militaristic stairway into the hell of thermonuclear destruction. I believe that unarmed truth and unconditional love will have the final word in reality. This is why right temporarily defeated is stronger than evil triumphant. ...

I have the audacity to believe that peoples everywhere can have three meals a day for their bodies, education and culture for their minds, and dignity, equality and freedom for their spirits. I believe that what self-centered men have torn down, men other-centered can build up. I still believe that one day mankind will bow before the altars of God and be crowned triumphant over war and bloodshed, and nonviolent redemptive goodwill will proclaim the rule of the land.

"And the lion and the lamb shall lie down together and every man shall sit under his own vine and fig tree and none shall be afraid." ...

MONTH

History can only move
towards liberty. History
can only have justice at
its heart. To march in
the opposite direction to
history is to be on the
road to shame, poverty
and oppression.

❦

Oscar Arias Sánchez

*The Nobel Foundation 1987

It often requires more
courage to dare to
do right than to fear
to do wrong.

≈

Abraham Lincoln

It seems to take more
courage to say NO to
war than to say YES.

≈

Aung San Suu Kyi

War may sometimes be a necessary evil. But no matter how necessary, it is always an evil, never a good. We will not learn how to live together in peace by killing each other's children.

Jimmy Carter

To live through traumatic events is not enough; one has to share them and transform them into acts of conscience.

≈

Elie Weisel

Civilization is a stream
with banks. The stream
is sometimes filled with
blood from people
killing, stealing, shouting
and doing the things
historians usually record,
while on the banks,
unnoticed, people build
homes, make love, raise
children, sing songs,
write poetry and even
whittle statues. The story
of civilization is the story
of what happened on
the banks. Historians are
pessimists because they
ignore the banks
for the river.

Will Durant

Fear is not the natural
state of civilized man.

Dag Hammarskjöld

Oscar Arias Sánchez

Former President of Costa Rica
From his Nobel Lecture given in Oslo, December 11, 1987

Peace consists, very largely, in the fact of desiring it with all one's soul. The inhabitants of my small country, Costa Rica, have realized those words by Erasmus. Mine is an unarmed people, whose children have never seen a fighter or a tank or a warship. ...

My country is a country of teachers. It is therefore a country of peace. We discuss our successes and failures in complete freedom. Because our country is a country of teachers, we closed the army camps, and our children go with books under their arms, not with rifles on their shoulders. We believe in dialogue, in agreement, in reaching a consensus. We reject violence. Because my country is a country of teachers, we believe in convincing our opponents, not defeating them. We prefer raising the fallen to crushing them, because we believe that no one possesses the absolute truth. Because mine is a country of teachers, we seek an economy in which men cooperate in a spirit of solidarity, not an economy in which they compete to their own extinction. ...

Hope is the strongest driving force for a people. Hope which brings about change, which produces new realities, is what opens man's road to freedom. Once hope has taken hold, courage must unite with wisdom. That is the only way of avoiding violence, the only way of maintaining the calm one needs to respond peacefully to offences.

MONTH

If there is to be peace
in the world,
There must be peace
in the nations.
If there is to be peace
in the nations,
There must be peace
in the cities.
If there is to be peace
in the cities,
There must be peace
between neighbors.
If there is to be peace
between neighbors,
There must be peace
in the home.
If there is to be peace
in the home,
There must be peace
in the heart.

Lao Tzu

I know God will not
give me anything I can't
handle. I just wish
that He didn't trust
me so much.

Mother Teresa

When I despair,
I remember that all
through history the
ways of truth and love
have always won. There
have been tyrants, and
murderers, and for a
time they can seem
invincible, but in the
end they always fall.
Think of it – always.

Gandhi

If everyone demanded
peace instead of
another television set,
then there'd be peace.

John Lennon

Courage is not simply
one of the virtues.
Courage is the form
of every virtue at its
testing point.

C.S. Lewis

Courage is the price
that Life exacts for
granting peace.

Amelia Earhart

I am fundamentally an
optimist. Part of being
optimistic is keeping
one's head pointed
toward the sun, one's
feet moving forward.
There were many dark
moments when my faith
in humanity was sorely
tested, but I would not
give myself up
to despair.

Nelson Mandela

a prayer for action

We cannot merely pray to God to end war;
For the world was made in a such a way
That we must find our own path of peace
If we could only find it within ourselves and our neighbors.

We cannot merely pray to God to root out prejudice;
For we already have eyes
With which to see the good in all people
If we would only judge them rightly.

We cannot merely pray to God to end starvation;
For we already have the resources
With which to feed the entire world
If we would only use them wisely.

We cannot merely pray to God to end despair;
For we already have the power
To clear away slums and to give hope
If we would only use our power justly.

We cannot merely pray to God to end disease;
For we already have great minds
With which to search out cures and healings
If we would only use them constructively.

Therefore we pray instead
For strength, determination, and willpower,
To do instead of merely to pray;
To become instead of merely to wish;
That our world may be safe,
And that our lives may be blessed.

Ken yehi ratzon, v'nomar Amen.
May it be so.

Rabbi Jack Reimer
Founding Chairperson of the National Rabbinic Network

The Universal "Golden Rule"

As ye would that men should do to you, do ye also to them.
The Bible, Luke 6:31

Do not to others what ye do not wish done to yourself.
This is the whole of righteousness – heed it well.
The Mahabharata, Hindu epic (ca. 5th c. BC)

That which is good for all and any one, for whomsoever – that is
good for me. …What I hold good for self, I should for all.
Zoroaster, Persian prophet (ca. 10th – 11th c. BC)

Do not do to others as you would not like done to yourself.
Confucius, sage of China (6th – 5th c. BC)

Do not to thy neighbor that thou wouldst not be done by him.
Pittacus of Lesbos, one of the Seven Sages of Greece (6th c. BC)

None of you [truly] believes until he wishes for his brother
what he wishes for himself.
The Prophet Mohammed (6th – 7th c. AD)

Hurt not others in ways that you yourself would find hurtful.
Buddhist teaching (9th – 10th c. AD)

What is hateful to thee, do not unto thy fellow man. This is the whole of the Law. The rest is but commentary.
Hillel the Elder, Jewish sage (1st c. BC – 1st c. AD)

All things are our relatives; what we do to everything, we do to ourselves. All is really One.
Black Elk, 19th c. Sioux spiritual leader

I define morality as adherence to the Golden Rule. "Do unto others as you would have them do unto you." If that is one's code of behavior, in my opinion, that person is moral. That is my code.

Barbara Jordan, 20th century educator, civil rights mentor and member of the U.S. House of Representatives

Peace Resources

Many of those whose words appear in this Journal are actively involved in organizations that promote the culture of peace. Here are just a few of the countless groups that embrace the ideals within these pages:

The Carter Center is committed to advancing human rights and alleviating unnecessary human suffering through its extensive peace-making and health programs. Visit www.cartercenter.org.

The Desmond Tutu Peace Foundation works in collaboration with the Desmond Tutu Peace Centre and Peace Trust to support the creation of a worldwide culture of peace through its reconciliation, non-violence and ethical leadership programs. Visit www.tutufoundation-usa.org.

Doctors Without Borders/Médecins Sans Frontières is an independent international organization that provides emergency medical aid around the world to people harmed by war, conflict, epidemics, disasters and exclusion from health care. Visit www.doctorswithoutborders.org.

The Elie Wiesel Foundation for Humanity is dedicated to combating indifference, intolerance and injustice through international dialogue and youth-focused programs. Visit www.eliewieselfoundation.org

The Green Belt Movement provides income and sustenance to millions of people in Kenya through the planting of trees. It also conducts educational campaigns to raise awareness about women's rights, civic empowerment and the environment throughout Kenya and Africa.
Visit www.greenbeltmovement.org

The Gorbachev Foundation of North America promotes the spread of democracy and economic liberalization through its advocacy, research, policy-analysis and education programs. Visit www.gfna.net.

The Nelson Mandela Foundation (NMF) encourages the creation of strategic partnerships in the spirit of reconciliation, or ubuntu, and social justice. Its Centre of Memory and Dialogue provides a forum for dialogue about some of the most difficult subjects of our time.

The Peace People was founded in 1976 in response to the violence in Northern Ireland. They are committed to building a just and peaceful society through nonviolent means. Visit www.peacepeople.com.

The Rigoberta Menchú Tum Foundation works for the rights of indigenous peoples – focusing on education, the creation of productive infrastructures, and the political settlement of conflicts through dialogue, negotiations and peace agreements.

Southern Poverty Law Center (SPLC) was founded as a small civil rights law firm in 1971. It is most well known for its tolerance education programs and its investigations into hate groups such as the Klu Klux Klan.
Visit www.splcenter.org.

University for Peace was established in Costa Rica under a United Nations mandate. Its mission is to provide humanity with an institution of higher education that promotes tolerance, understanding and peaceful coexistence. Visit www.upeace.org.

Women for Women International mobilizes women to change their lives through a holistic approach to addressing the special needs of women in conflict and post-conflict environments. Through the organization's unique work, women achieve greater social, economic and political participation in their communities. Visit www.womenforwomen.org.

The soul is made of love
and must ever strive to return to love.

✿

Mechthild of Magdeburg